Adventures in
MARKETING
AUT⊙MATION

Out-of-the-box tips, concepts, and ideas on how to use
***Robotics**, **Artificial Intelligence**, and **Automation** to*
reach a wider audience.

FRANK DAPPAH

DEDICATION

Dedicated to Bernice. Thanks for the support.

WHY READ THIS BOOK

Read this little book of mine if you are a small business owner or entrepreneur, or perhaps you are looking to start a company, and are:

- Curious to know how marketing automation can help grow your business.

- Looking for some ideas on how to make your operations more efficient via automation.

- Looking for insights on which areas of your sales and marketing can benefit from automation

- Looking for information on the best tools to help put your marketing apparatus on autopilot

- Ideas on the best ways to automate your marketing

- Curious to know how effective Marketing Automation really is.

TABLE OF CONTENTS

1   LAWYERS AND FARMERS   14

2   THE POWER OF MORE   22

3   A (GLOBAL) RUSH TO AUTOMATE   28

4   WHY AUTOMATE?   34

5   SOCIAL MATIRX   43

6   A GOOD OLD FRIEND   58

7   PLAN, SEGMENT, PERSONALIZE   74

8   CHATBOTS, SMS, AND MORE   88

9   All-IN-ONE MARKETING AUTOMATION PLATFORMS   102

   AUTOMATION INTROSPECTIVA   117

   ABOUT THE AUTHOR   123

CHAPTER ONE

LAWYERS AND FARMERS

Ever wonder how large corporations are able to operate with such smoothness and precision? How do they do it?

Take **Europa Sports** for example. The Charlotte, NC- based nutritional supplements distributor, one of my favorite companies, with thousands of customers and various locations is still able to deliver their products on time, all day every day. They never make a mistake, it seems. I am serious.

At one of my companies, we work with Europa all the time. They ship out hundreds of customer orders and I must say, it is always as seamless as can be.

Another organization that has really mastered the art of effortless dependable operations is *Amazon*.

The fact that a company that big can deliver such quality customer service and logistics boggles the mind. Well, my mind at least.

These examples are not that of some kind of superhuman achievements, but rather a testament to the advancements in technology that has transpired over the last 10 to 15 years.

My wife and I recently laughed at the fact that *Wework Inc*. the shared office space operator was described as a "Technology Company" in their IPO filings. We thought, "how are they a technology outfit?"

Well, the joke's on us because if you really think about it, and I encourage you not to, you will come to realize that, in one way or another, all firms are tech-ish firms these days.

Sure, most business models function- for the most part - as they have since the establishment of these various verticals.

Lawyers are still lawyering and farmers still farm. The change here has to do with how they do what they do.

The Farmer now uses technology: GPS-guided, and internet-ready equipment to ensure output at a certain pace and of predictable quality.

The Lawyer? well, he or she now uses all kinds of gizmos to help manage a large client base and help deliver superior service.

Although, various kinds of tech help power the modern workplace, for the purpose of this book, I will focus on Automation, or more specifically Automation within your marketing system.

SCREAM IT FROM THE MOUNTAIN TOPS

We must tell people what we do, period. We can have the most innovative product, offer it at an enviable price, but fail to gain traction if no one knows about it.

If you have read any of my other books, you know then how often I stress the importance of building a system within your company to do precisely what I am talking about.

A robust system that exists only to identify the most suitable prospective customers for your products and services; and offer the opportunity for them to consume your offerings.

This system must be able to evolve, grow, and reach new targets in new markets all the time.

Sales and marketing should be on your mind all the time. You must eat and breath it. This is the only path to true growth.

It really makes no difference what kind of business you are in.

Whether Farmer or Lawyer, you must have a sales and marketing system in place. One that, while based on well-established principles and methods, is however powered by modern technologies.

This is the way to stay ahead of inevitable global competition.

A SYSTEM FOR THIS AND A SYSTEM FOR THAT

You, my friend, must seek to build systems within your company whenever you can. This is of the utmost importance. Start with the actions and tasks that are directly tied to your bottom line.

Those things that directly contribute to revenue, cash flow, and profitability. You stand to benefit greatly by taking these steps.

So, what are some of the things I speak of?
Customer support, product development, and yes,
sales and marketing.

These are the parts of your business that
simply cannot continue to function as random
sporadic occurrences within your organization. You
must be focused on improving and 10x-ing these
functions, especially if you are a solopreneur or work
with a small team.

Sure, you can outsource many tasks in your
business, but these tasks I am talking about should
never be left to a third party to handle.

AND WHILE YOU ARE AT IT

Look for every opportunity to Automate when you
can. That's right, seize the chance, use the latest
technologies to build semi-autonomous systems. Start
with your sales and marketing activities. Automate as
much of it as you can.

Of course, sales always needs the human
touch, I get that, but examine as much of your
marketing system as you can, looking for every
opportunity to use Automation to reach and serve
more and more people.

As I have stated before, this is the path to
growth and profitability.

This is how Wal-Mart does it. This is How
Amazon almost always gets your order right.

This is how the UPS delivers on time 99% of
the time.

Sure, these companies employ thousands of

folks to help make sure things run smoothly, but they also spend billions of dollars a year looking for new technologies to help automate as much as they can and help reduce cost while driving growth and profitability.

WHAT TO EXPECT

There is no doubt there is a need for organizations, big and small to be bigger, more profitable, and to do so in the most cost-effective ways possible. This is the way of Capitalism. This is what we do: More, better, faster, cheaper.

Among other things, we can accomplish these tasks and meet these expectations via automation.

Once thought to be futuristic or a luxury only enjoyed by larger entities, automation, more specifically, the technologies that facilitate, and drive automation are now available to small firms like yours and mine. This is in part due to the invention of the cloud and globalization, and an overall embrace of mobile technology, Robotics, and Artificial intelligence.

In this book, I will point to various everyday ways you - the small business owner can use automation to grow your company.

I will highlight some ways you can automate certain tasks in order to free up some of your time. Time better spent on more strategic tasks.

I will share some ideas and concepts to help

you think about marketing and automation in new ways. I shall also talk about the three most obvious, yet effective ways you can innovate within your marketing efforts and the benefits of creating automated systems around these three major marketing channels.

We will look at Automation in Email Marketing, Social media marketing, and direct (instant) customer communications.

I will share some of the strategies I use within my group of companies to help drive growth.

CHAPTER TWO

THE POWER OF MORE

MORE IS MORE PROFITABLE

The way I see it, the entire modern global economy is built on this very simple idea. Companies all over the world seek new sales and marketing opportunities all day long.

This is the reason business folk rack up so many frequent flyer miles year over year.

Everyone is constantly looking for new ways and places to sell more of their products and services.

This is the reason there is a McDonald's in almost every community in America, on every street corner, it seems; and most of the developed world.

This is the reason Hollywood creates movies, these days, not just for U.S audiences but for a global community.

Movie makers must now consider the reception of their works on a global scale. They must consider how audiences in Nairobi, or Accra will feel about certain scenes and statements.

And as we seek to sell more to more people, we must find ways to streamline the entire process.

WHAT WOULD WAL-MART DO (WWWD)

Very few American companies do " More" better

than Wal-Mart. Year after year, The Bentonville, Arkansas company delivers the untold profits that can only be realized at the intersection of volume and efficiency via automation and innovation, even in the mundane retail sector.

What started out as a small bargain retailer in 1962, today boasts $514.4 billion in annual sales, 2.2 million employees worldwide, with operations in more than 27 countries.

The company has managed to expand their operations and product offerings while adhering to the promise of Low-priced items.

They have done this by integrating automation in most of their operations. From supply chain management, to sales and marketing, Wal-Mart employs various automated technological systems and processes to expand their brand while controlling cost.

ROBOTIC BARISTA

It is hard to imagine another coffee chain that yields as much power, and with as much brand recognition as Starbucks. The green mermaid logo has become synonyms with coffee all over the world.

I know it is hard to imagine, but there were other coffee houses before Starbucks, but I bet you cannot name a single one.

The history of coffee in North America can be divided into before Starbucks (BS), and after Starbucks (AS).

Just like any other global corporate giant, the Seattle-based coffee chain has embraced Artificial intelligence and Automation, along with savvy marketing and an ever-expanding real estate portfolio to expand its global footprint.

With the help of companies like The Ammunition Group, the design company behind Dr. Dre's Beats by Dre Headphones, the Seattle-based company is planning to roll out Cafe X Technologies, a new automated barista.

Once implemented, the $25,000 robotic arm will be able to make up to 120 cups of coffee per hour.

The Company hopes to be able to serve more people faster with this new tech. This is just one example of how Starbucks and companies like it are looking to fully embrace automation in all aspects of their operations.

Cafe X

PREACHING TO THE CHOIR

As we look at how automation, robotics, artificial intelligence has transformed the modern workforce, let us further tether - for the sake of this book - our concepts and views to that of the needs of today's entrepreneur, The Small business operator and other folks like her. Business folk who may not have the billions of dollars in operating cash that Wal-Mart or Starbucks may have, but yet, stand to benefit from the use of automated systems.

How does this shift to automation affect you? Well, seeing as most small businesses are started by folks with little to no money, it helps that we capitalize on every technological advantage we can. Mostly to increase and improve productivity.

With the help of platforms like SendinBlue, Hubspot, you too can take advantage of the power of more.

CHAPTER THREE

A (GLOBAL) RUSH TO AUTOMATE

In Chapter One, I talked about the need for you, the Small business entrepreneur to create systems around the activities within your company that have a direct effect on your financial health as a company.

I talked about the need to create robust systems around Sales and Marketing and other detrimental activities/divisions within your firm.

CHANGE COMETH

Here, I want to take this idea a step further. Once you are able to create systems around these activities that directly impact your profitability, I encourage you to look for ways to maximize efficiencies. There is a need to automate as much as possible, the activities that are repetitive in nature.

Especially the ones that require perfect, or near-perfect execution each time. Among many positives, Automation, even at the small business level will go a long way to help you reduce cost and will help your company stay competitive. That's right: competitive.

I am sure by now, with all the news coverage out there, including Democratic presidential candidate, Andrew Yang's book: *The War on Normal People: The Truth About America's*

Disappearing Jobs and Why Universal Basic Income Is Our Future, you are aware of the changes automation is causing around the world. Almost every small town across America has been greatly impacted by automation and the proliferation of robotics and AI in the workplace.

EMBRACE CHANGE

Now, I am more in the "embrace the change" camp on this particular issue. I am of this opinion for many reasons. Reasons I'd rather not go into. I, however, believe that since these changes are going to occur whether we like it or not, there is a need for small business owners and entrepreneurs such as yourself to equip themselves with the knowledge and resources to stay ahead of this trend. You can also compete with the "big guys" if you learn to embrace, and most importantly, invest in some of the tools and technologies that give said big guys the advantage. These tools are available to you as well.

As you read this book, right now, companies all over the world are taking the necessary steps to integrate Robotics, AI, and other Automated technology systems to help them reduce cost and increase profits.

AUTOMATION BY THE NUMBERS

Automation is happening all over the world. Most companies are, in one way or another investing significantly in automated technologies.

Marketing Automation statistics

On average 51% of companies are currently using Marketing automation. With more than half of B2B companies (58%) plan to adopt the technology
75% of marketers say they currently use at least one type of marketing automation tools. Making automation tools accepted by most marketers.

Spending for Marketing Automation tools will grow vigorously over the next few years, reaching $25.1 billion annually by 2023 from $11.4 billion in 2017.

55% of marketing decision-makers plan to increase their spending on Marketing Technology, with one-fifth of the respondents expecting to increase by 10 percent or more. 38% will spend the same, while only 8% decreases their spend

Marketers say the most important objectives of a marketing automation strategy are:

- Optimizing productivity (43%)
- Increasing marketing ROI (41%)
- Improving campaign management (40%)
- Improving database quality (39%)
- Acquiring more customers (39%)

- Measuring performance (37%)
- Aligning Marketing and Sales (24%)

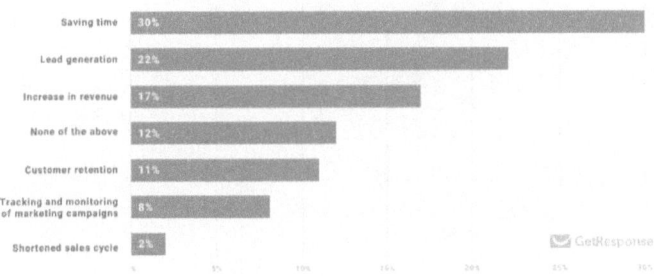

JUST THE TIP OF THE ICEBUIRG

As you can see, companies and other Organizations all over the world have either invested in Marketing Automation systems or are looking to take Marketing automation seriously.

Companies both large and small have come to realize the need to Automate portions of their marketing systems in an effort to reduce cost significantly and increase profitability.

CHAPTER FOUR

WHY AUTOMATE?

Short answer? We automate to realize "the power of more" We use cheaper, more efficient systems. Systems that can essentially run on their own because we want more. We automate to be able to do more. Work les but produce more. Be more predictable. Be a bit more consistent.

We want to spend less on – in this case, Sales and Marketing so we can make more money. More profits, more output, more customers, more stores, you get the idea.

If you are looking at Automation as a way to streamline your company's marketing efforts and to boost overall return on investment, it is imperative that you take the time to understand what Marketing automation really is and the benefits associated with it.

On a basic level, Marketing automation comes down to efficiency.

The primary reason you will want to automate some of the repetitive tasks associated with your Sales & marketing infrastructure is to ensure that your employees' time and efforts are efficiently distributed across all departments in order of priority.

In this chapter, we will take a holistic look at what Marketing automation is and its benefits.

BENEFITS OF MARKETING AUTOMATION

As I mentioned before, the main reason behind automation, not just when it comes to marketing, but across all industries is to streamline some of the more repetitive actions associated with your business.

Doing so will help you reduce the opportunity for human error, reduce your overhead costs, and so much more.

So, just briefly: Automation is the use of technology to autonomously perform certain tasks without a whole lot of human supervision or input.

For the most part, automating some of your marketing messages, campaigns and tasks will go a long way to:

Streamline your marketing processes

One of the major benefits of Marketing automation is the ability to visualize and build panoramic customer journeys.

You are able to create a series of campaigns/messages/content that will help walk every single customer through a customized process designed to anticipate and remedy any issues they may have and educate them about your brand in the most thorough way possible.

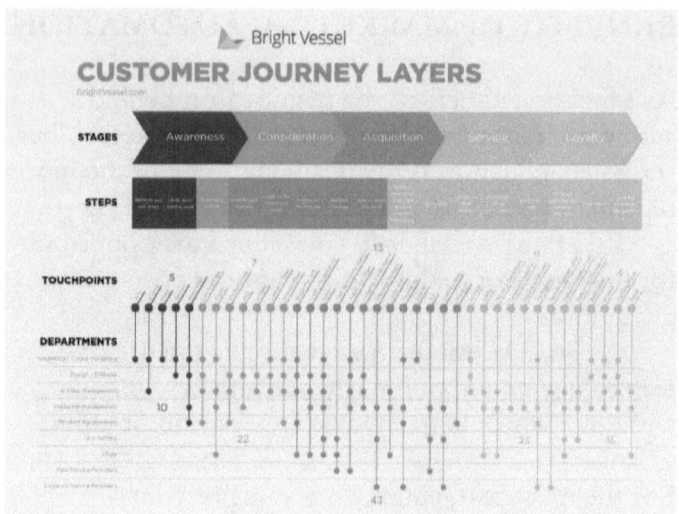

Retain and Increase the Value of Existing Customers

Other than serving as a means by which you can help provide quality effortless customer service, marketing automation when executed in an optimal fashion can be one of the most effective tools in your sales toolbox.

The ability to get in front of the customer, via email, social media, push notifications, etc. With your brand messaging can provide you with a powerful sales platform.

You can help convert more free trial users and upsell existing customers through the attention you will commend with your ubiquitous and consistent messaging.

Targeted Marketing

Through the use of the various tools and features most all-in-one marketing automation platforms provide, you will be able to speak directly to each customer's unique needs and wants.

You will be able to deploy ultra-targeted messages. These customized messages will help provide your customers with the world-class support they have come to expect, and also help increase their spending with your company by providing a message of value that resonates with each individual customer on a granular level.

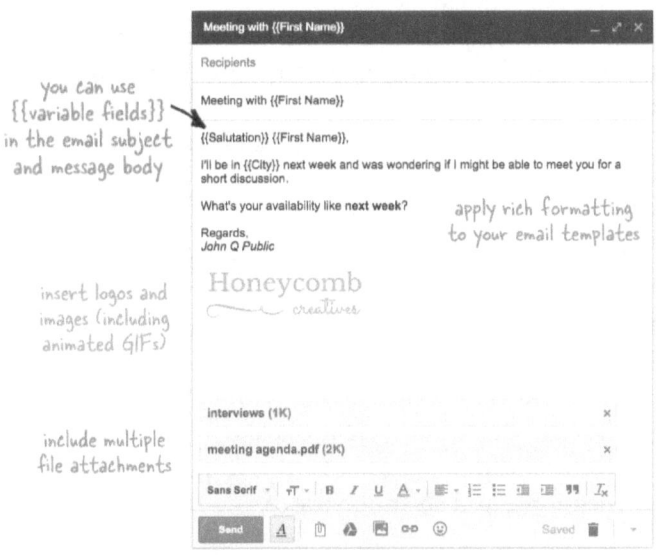

Automatically follow-up with leads

According to a study by the Harvard Business Review, you are 60x more likely to qualify, and subsequently, close a sale if you follow up with a lead within an hour of them expressing interest in your product or service.

And since it is almost impossible to respond to a slew of information requests or free trial users as quickly as possible, it makes sense to employ the use of some of the various marketing automation tools out there to help keep up with incoming leads.

You will be able to build and execute, via triggers, responses to leads to help qualify them, and set them up for the next step in your sales process.

If you operate a software business or online magazine or blog, you can send out automated welcome emails with video demos on how to use your platform to help your free trial users get the most out of your system before they upgrade to a paid account.

You are also able to automatically engage and provide customers with the information required to better understand the value of your product or service.

You can communicate with customers and prospective customers via tools like Tidio, using chatbots, automated social media responses, in-app notifications, and so much more.

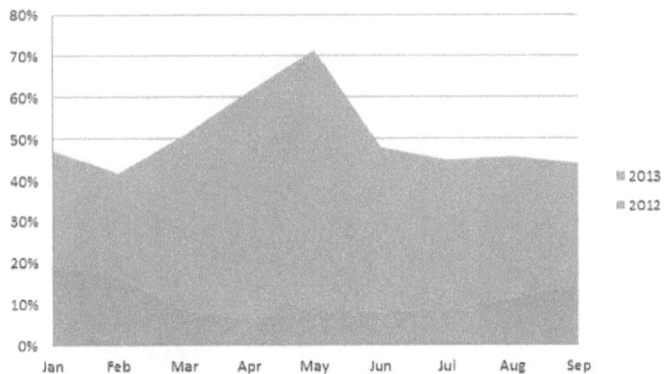

Capterra

Sales Qualification Rate
Before and After Marketing Automation

Analytics

Marketing automation and the associated tools and features will help give you an overview of the effectiveness of your marketing efforts.

Your reporting dashboard will give you great transparency and insights as to which campaigns are resonating with your audience, which campaigns are leading to greater conversation rates, and so on.

Armed with this information, you will be able to better streamline your overall marketing strategy.

A Customized System

These are but a few of the benefits of Marketing automation. I am sure, just like most business operators, once you have a much better understand and appreciation for the power of automation, you will be able to come up with strategies that are unique to your business.

I have no doubt in your ability to build and put into place, an automated marketing system that will help meet your specific business needs.

One that will help educate your prospective customers while keeping your existing base engaged.

CHAPTER FIVE

SOCIAL MATRIX

The dynamic nature of the ever-expanding social media landscape provides endless marketing opportunities for organizations of varying sizes and types.

From Fortune 500 multi-national conglomerates to local mom-and-pop retailers, all kinds of firms can find and engage global audiences via the power of social media.

One of the truly remarkable powers of social media - besides the large user base and connectivity, is the diversity of types of content that can be disseminated across multiple platforms to folks in many countries.

For the purpose of Content Marketing, platforms like Facebook and Instagram lay the groundwork for marketers to share text, video, photos, and so much more.

I believe that Social media, from a small business owner's perspective, as a tool to help reach new audiences is probably the most powerful development in marketing over the last 20 years. Very few media channels rival the power and reach of social media.

Taken together, the various social media networks out there provide even the most cash-strapped entrepreneur with a real means to connect and tell the whole world about their products and services.

Firms like Kabbage and Podio have found millions of users for their products by investing heavily in social media marketing.

In this chapter, we shall walk through some of the benefits of social media marketing, the various tools to help you put your social media marketing efforts in auto drive and the benefits of automation in the area.

But first, let's consider the current state of social media marketing automation.

AUTOMATION IN MOTION

Social media automation essentially is the use of various tools and platforms to help create, and to a larger extent automate or semi-automate the distribution of your content across multiple social media platforms.

Most social media automation tools like Hootuite or Sprout will go a log way to help you simultaneously share content on Facebook, Twitter, Instagram, and the rest of the major social networks.

Automation will also help build your brand due to the fact that by automating some or most of your content / posts, you will bring much needed consistency to your content distribution systems and processes.

Consistency is crucial to the success of any social media campaign.

You will also be able to get up and running

with any type of campaign due to the user-friendly interface most social media automation platforms are known for.

My favorite: Onlywire (www.onlywire.com) has a smooth, easy-to-use design, which allows me to build and send posts in minutes.

Social media automation will also help you grow, not just your social media presence but your entire brand reach as a result of consistent automated posts.

YOU ARE NOT ALONE

The whole world, it seems – well, the business world has come to realize the greatness of the opportunity that exists in social media.

I mean, never before has there been such an inexpensive, yet powerful way to reach new folks and engage "old" ones.

T.V gave us the chance, as marketers and business owners to connect with folks when they got home from work.

Stay-at-home Moms tuned in during the day, given marketers the opportunity to connect with them via Soaps and other dynamic daytime programming.

Radio got to you on your drive to and from work, the Store, or wherever you were headed.

But social media + "Mobile" gives us a chance to reach people 24/7 wherever they may be.

At the gym, at school, at work, consumers are always on these social media platforms.

This opportunity has not gone unnoticed by companies around the world. Facebook alone has been able to build a very profitable business by providing businesses with the chance to market their stuff to consumers all around the world, and the Social media giant's arsenal of marketing tools is especially useful if you sell products or services that can be consumed regardless of one's geographical location.

Facebook has also been able to build various marketing programs to help local businesses connect with and attract consumers in their communities.

Other platforms have also managed to conjure up innovative ways to help their business users hit their marketing goals.

Social media marketing, as segment of the marketing universe is on an upswing. Even political groups have gotten in on the actions.

Social media spend is now a big pat of any politicians' marketing budgets.

THE NUMBERS

If you take a quick look at the statistics associated with social marketing and social media automation, you will find that:

- 77% of consumers are likely to buy products and services from brands they follow on Social media.
- 75% of consumers like when brands use humor in their social media posts/campaigns
- 86% of consumers say they want brands to be

honest when it comes to how they interact with them on social media

- 83 % of consumers and Facebook users prefer brands to show personality within their posts and other types of content they share.
- 75% of consumers believe there's value in brands exhibiting humor on social, only 36% are willing to purchase from brands they believe are funny.
- 40% of consumers don't want to see personality from Government agencies on social.

NOW YOU KNOW

Judging by these numbers, I am sure you are thinking of several ways in which you can capitalize and maximize on the enormous opportunity that social media provides.

I am sure you have thought of many ways through which you can capture the attention of your desired audience and turn a portion of them into fans, clients, users, customers, etc.

You can create a formidable content / social media marketing strategy across most of the major social media apps via constant, consistent sharing of valuable content and the power of automation.

A MULTI-PLATFORM APPROACH

As you look to grow your business and look to streamline your marketing efforts, you are better served by approaching social media from a dynamic perspective.

You can reach audiences on various different platforms using engaging content.

You can provide the information needed at the right time via the use of various social automation platforms like Hootsuite and Onlywire.

These apps have the features you will need to plan, setup and deploy an effective automated social media campaign.

QUALITY CONTENT

When it comes to social media marketing, Content is everything. What type of content you choose to share with your audience can determine whether they completely ignore your brand or are fully engaged with your posts.

Sure, different types of content resonate with different kinds of audiences in different ways. The key here is to find out which types of content will work for your particular set of needs.

Taken independently, audiences have been known to respond to some types of content in a more optimal fashion than others.

According to Sprout Social, 48% of consumers say they want to purchase from brands that are responsive to their customers on social media and 38% will buy from brands that share "interesting visuals" on their social media pages.

Once you find your perfect mix of articles, videos, and / photos, you will want to only use the most captivating, top quality and fully immersive selection of content.

Sharing quality, target-audience-friendly content will help audiences engage with your brand, come to see your firm as the go-to folks for whatever you sell, and help increase overall customer engagement.

Your social media content strategy should not be left to chance. This is what audiences will come to expect and know your company for. Take your time to plan out what types of content, what themes - introspective, activist, humor, etc. You will be known for.

For example, GEICO, Warren Buffett's insurance firm stays at the top of the mind due to their consistently funny ads and unforgettable visuals. I still remember their contaminated water supply ad from the '90s. That's how funny this ad was. Well, to me at least.

A CLEAR PATH TO YES
Starts with a well-planned social media marketing campaign. **YES**, in this context refers to getting your targeted audience to take the actions you need.

Whether it is reading a blog post, starting a free trial on your site.

There has to be a point, an endgame to your social media marketing efforts.

SUCCESS here will be heavily dependent on how well you plan your campaign. For any social media campaign to be effective, you will need to carefully examine.

Your Ultimate Goal- When it's all said and done,

what would like folks to do with your content? Are you simply looking to drive traffic to your new site or blog? Or do you want folks who try your software app to upgrade to a paid account? What do you want them to do, ultimately?

This point is very important to think about as it will help you build the perfect customer journeys.

Ones that match the behavior of each prospect group on each social media platform. What do I mean by that? Well, you know, most folks on, say LinkedIn are going to be serious, straight-to-the-point professional types, while courting prospects on Twitter or Instagram might require a bit more finessing.

The idea is to establish an ultimate goal and then curate each campaign to fit each social media platform.

Customer Journey

We all have some idea of what we want folks to do when we approach them with our offer(s). We know if we want them to buy a product, read a blog post, subscribe to a newsletter, etc.

The thing is, if you have been in business for any considerable amount of time, you know that the path to "Yes", "yes, I will read your article"; "yes, I will start a free trial on your platform", is never a straight one.

We start with a large group of prospects, then move them through a series of steps, with most deciding not to follow through.

We finally get a percentage of a percentage of the number we started with to take that final step we need.

This process, the process of moving your prospects through various deliberate qualifying steps is your customer journey.

These are the various steps customers take to get to "yes". I think it is very important to plan your customer journeys and automate most of them. Sure, you might want to put a warm body on the closing of sales in some instances, but for the most part, you will want to automate a majority of the steps you lay out for customers to take till they give their ultimate buy-in.

Each step, whether the initial introduction of your product on social media or perhaps an offer of a free whitepaper should always have clear calls-to-action.

You will want to use beautifully produced social media content and clear language to entice your audience to follow the path you have laid out.

Video or bust

Allow me to reiterate that your social media campaign lives or dies based on the type of content you use. I kid you not. I know this may sound a bit dramatic, but this is a fact. Different types of audiences in different geographies respond differently to different types of content.

Needless to say, the social media landscape regardless of which platform you use isn't one built for long-form reading so it is best not to make your ads too text-heavy.

Video, when selling visual products and services works best. It is best to dig a little deeper into any type of research material out there to see which types of content will work best for your type of business.

You can also simply do a careful analysis of what types of content your closest, most successful competitor uses. See which types of content they use for which types of ads. You will be surprised how much you can figure out about what works in your industry by checking-out what the "winners" in your space are doing to stay ahead of the game.

According to social media research agency, Social Monday, one must either inspire folks with their content, get folks to think, or motivate emotionally to build momentum on social media.

The five types of content through which you can communicate any one of the discussed ideas are eBooks, interactive content, positive content-emotional motivation is best when done in a positive way, user-generated content, or visual content.

Video is still king of all content as far as social media is concerned. Video resonates across all platforms and countries.

According to wyzowl (www.wyzowl.com), 87% of businesses now use video as a marketing tool. 96% of people say they've watched an explainer video to learn more about a product or service.

79% of people say a brand's video has convinced them to buy a piece of software or app. 68% of people say they'd most prefer to learn about a new product or service by watching a short video.

This makes video more popular as a learning tool than text-based articles (15%), infographics (4%) presentations and pitches (4%) eBooks and manuals (3%).

Social Media Video Engagement Roundup:

Online browsers, shoppers, etc. Enjoy video more than any other type of content - 85% of internet users in the United States watched online video content across all their devices.

A recent spike in demand for more video content by consumers is causing more and more brands to find ways to make video a big part of their social media, and overall digital marketing plan. Even companies that have never considered themselves "videoable" must now face the reality that they must "video" or be left behind. According to Hubspot, 54% of consumers want to see more video content from brands they support and/ or follow on social media.

Video has also been a great way for marketers, big and small to inexpensively attract new customers. The relevantly quick ramp up of video as compared to other marketing campaigns has also gone a long way to help brands of all sizes seize the opportunity to create highly effective, yet budget-friendly content to share online. Wyzowl reports that 87% of marketers use video as a marketing tool.

Social media was made for video. Or maybe it's the other way around? Either way, consumers love video on social. According to Animoto, Video ranks as the number one preferred type of content consumers prefer on social media. Consumers specifically prefer to see video content as the main way in which their favorite brands present new ideas, product, and service offerings to them.

Video is great at producing handsome returns. According to Animoto, 88% of small business owners and Marketers are satisfied with the ROI of their video marketing efforts on social media.

Video is also a great way to generate quality sales leads. There are many reasons why Marketers are increasingly warming up to the idea of using social media as a lead generation tool. The most significant of these reasons is the ease of use of various social media platforms, the effectiveness of videos and the details most social media apps provide as far as their users go. Optinmonster reports that Video Marketers get 66% more qualified leads per year.

Posting Schedule

Pick posting times and triggers that work well, not just for you and your business but more importantly for your audience. This makes huge difference. Just like how location is the key to real estate success, timing is everything to social media marketing success and even when it comes to email marketing. I am sure you have some ideas why. The average person is constantly being bombarded by all kinds of information. From new alerts that seem to want to scare the crap out of everyone, I mean, is it really "breaking news" if it happened two days ago? Anyway, to allow your audience to actually see your content, you must pick times that fit into their daily lives. Business folks, entrepreneurs, small business owners, etc. Are more likely to see and interact with your posts early in the A.M before 7. Consumers can be reached after dinner, 7 PM-ish.

Platform
Choose a social media automation platform that works best for you. There are some awesome ones out there, most of which I have tried. I think Hootsuite has a great platform, so does Sprout. Each platform has its own set of features, some unique and others common. The key for me, since I rely heavily on automation to create the 10x factor, is to find one that has a mix of automation tools, but also works well with the resources available to me. And by resources, I mean money. I currently use Onlywire (https://onlywire.com) and Outpost (https://outpostsocial.com). Onlywire, in my opinion offers the most bang for my buck, in that I get to commandeer and post to a wide variety of platforms beyond Facebook, Twitter, and Instagram. Outpost on the other hand provides more flexibility and control over my automation systems.

CHAPTER SIX

A GOOD OLD FRIEND

As you continue to grow your business, I am sure you have become all too familiar with occupying many different titles. By now you know that you are sometimes the Chief Marketing officer of your business, and other times you have to wear the hat of the Chief Technology Officer.

Well, such is the life of an entrepreneur. Regardless of whether you operate a small business, and I mean really small, or you have a few more members on your team than usual, you will have to learn to perform many functions, and well. The role of the marketing overseer should be navigated with all the seriousness it deserves.

One such element of marketing that should be mastered is email. Email marketing, an oldie but goodie, should be one of your main channels through which you embark on the task of communicating your value proposition with your target audience.

In this chapter, we shall address some of the roles email can play to help elevate your marketing strategy and uncover some of the reasons email marketing is still one of the most efficient and powerful ways to present your brand to the world.

We will also address the need automate your email marketing system best you can and the reasons and benefits of email marketing automation.

EMAIL MARKETING LIVES ON

I caution you to not get distracted by all the other (shiny) new forms of marketing out there. I like to tell folks to rather employ a multifaceted approach when it comes to marketing.

You are better served if you choose a handful of marketing options and carefully craft an overall marketing approach that seeks to incorporate all the marketing tools and platforms to help drive home a single message.

Your message. When it comes to digital marketing and marketing automation, email should occupy a place at the top of the heap. Do not play around with your email marketing system.

Here is why:

Just ask ROI
Most small business owners and marketers identify Email marketing as their biggest source of customers. In fact, 59% of marketers say email provides the largest share of ROI.

With email, most marketers get a chance to reach the greatest number of prospective customers for the least amount or share of overall marketing budgets.

Where it leads
Email marketing is and has always been the number one source of leads for sales professionals all around

the world. Email (even on a smaller scale) goes hand-in-hand with lead generation. The sheer reach of email and its low cost to set up makes email marketing a businessperson's best friend when it comes to marketing.

Marketers, small business folk, and sales professionals all use email as their primary method by which they generate leads for their businesses. According to Sprout social, 89% of marketers say email serves as their primary channel for lead generation.

Audience size

Experts project the use of email to grow exponentially by 2021. There are currently over 3.7 billion active email users in the world. That is correct, email use has actually grown over the last ten years despite the introduction and heavy usage of other forms of communication. Social media, text messaging, instant messaging, etc.

Never actually replaced email. All these tools now work well together with your email as well as phone communications, and if you are in business then you know how important it is to provide many channels of communication between you and your customers.

Email use will actually reach 4.1 billion by 2021. Smartphones and a whole host of other tech tools have helped fuel the growth in usage of email.

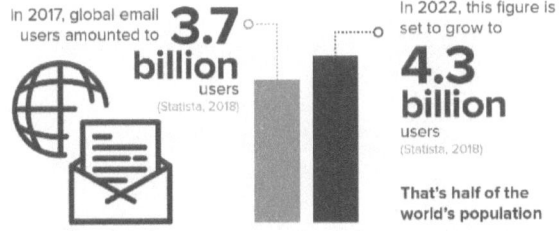

In 2017, global email users amounted to **3.7 billion users** (Statista, 2018)

In 2022, this figure is set to grow to **4.3 billion users** (Statista, 2018)

That's half of the world's population

It's mobile

Smartphones and the ubiquity of mobile apps have been a godsend to the email marketer and small business owner/entrepreneur. She no longer has to wait for folks to see her promotional ads when they sit at their computers to check their emails. Nope! folks will now see your campaigns pop up right there on their mobile devices.

And since we all carry these devices everywhere and can't seem to take our eyes off their screens, you do not have to worry that your email marketing campaigns will go unnoticed.

According to email marketing firm Litmus, over 60% of all email opens happen on a mobile device. That is over half of the population of email users.

Litmus also adds that 28% of all emails are read on an iPhone and the most popular email app is Google's Gmail app.

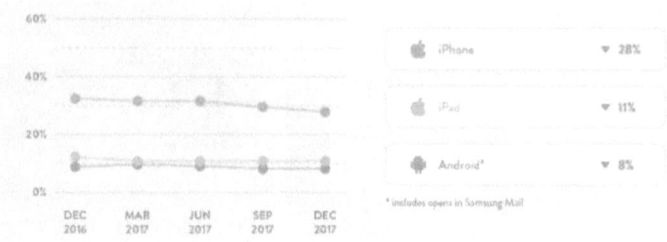

New developments

This next statement may seem strange to some but " there are new tech tools in the email marketing world". Yup, just like in other technology-based fields, there are a whole host of new and future systems that insiders believe will help small business owners, marketers, and entrepreneurs better connect with their audiences via email.

One such innovation is "Interactive emails". Many believe that email marketers of tomorrow will help give themselves a leg-up if they adopt, among many things, emails that readers/ audiences can interact with. It is not enough to segment and personalize your emails anymore.

Video, for example, is one of the types of content emerging as an ROI booster in email marketing. In fact, according to Martech Advisor, adding videos to your email campaigns will help boost your open rates by 300%. Adding other forms of new media like sliders, collapsible menus, and GIFs will help make your emails more appealing to audiences, especially if your products and services are designed to attract younger customers.

SUMMER MENU   CHEF'S SPECIALS   NEW AT PRET   PRET RECIPES

ICE-COLD ~ FRESHLY BLENDED

• FRAPPES & FRUIT SMOOTHIES •

OUR SUMMER DRINKS ›

f 🐦 📷

63

AN AUTOMATABLE STRATEGY

I am pretty sure by telling all the advantages of email marketing and providing all these glowing stats, I am preaching to the choir here.

If you bought this book, then I am pretty sure you already know how powerful email marketing is and how email can help you reach new customers. I am sure you already know all this. You bought this little book of mine to learn how to best automate your communications to help make you more efficient and your business more profitable.

This is why you bought this book; I am sure. That being said, let's take a look at some well-replicated and well-received email marketing automation strategies out there, some that I have put in place myself to help grow my company.

Before we do though, I don't want you to think of email marketing as just a form of marketing. I want you to look at your entire communications system as one giant language with email, social media, and all other channels as simply dialects. Just different ways (all belonging to one big language) through which you communicate with your audience.

The message remains the same, with just tweaks to how you "say" it. The purpose of this book is to identify some of the most spoken dialects and think about how to amplify and automate your voice to connect with the most people possible.

A welcoming face

Regardless of what type of business you are in, when it comes to automation in your email marketing, you should pay very close attention to your "welcome message".

I know this may seem like a simple idea. A no-brainer even, but no, the Welcome email is one of the most important automated email messages you will ever send.

This is for many reasons, the least of which is the likelihood that your prospect will definitely open your welcome email. Once automated to be sent immediately, your welcome email will help set the tone for all other email communications that will follow.

Audiences, via your welcome email, will have a mental imprint of your brand. They will take note of your URL and other brand graphics, leading to future opens.

According to Get Response, the average open rate for welcome emails is 82%.

Research also shows that your new user or subscriber is more likely to open your welcome email if sent out within the first hour of their subscription or interaction with your website.

Audiences tend to move on if you wait too long to send your welcome email.

For this reason, it is highly critical that you fully automate all welcome emails to be sent out "immediately". Within your welcome email should be very clear and simple instructions (other than your heartwarming message) on what your new prospect can expect.

It helps not to bombard your new user with

too much information. Simply segment and personalize your email to anticipate what your new user's one question will be and answer it.

Server-level shenanigans

If you operate an online-only type of business, say a Software-as-a-service firm or an eCommerce business, then it is safe to assume that most, if not all your customers/users will find and buy your stuff online, via their desktop computers or mobile devices. Am I right? This makes online marketing your primary tool in the pursuit of new customers.

It is always a good idea to connect with apps like Constant Contact and Benchmark to setup, segment and automate your email communications with your new users and customers.

These popular email marketing clients will help you set up your [sending domain] and customize a bunch of email templates to be sent out at different times of your interactions with your customers. And although these tools offer a whole host of customizations tools as well as features to help you reach your audience's inbox, it can sometimes become difficult to do just that.

This is because, as you send out more and more promotional emails, most email service providers like Google and Microsoft will start to identify your domain as a "commercial" one. Yup, Google is onto you and your B.S. I have found the it helps to work with a software developer to help you send a few emails at the server level.

Sure, it will cost you a couple of bucks to do

so if you do not know how to code yourself, but it is well worth it. Now I am not asking you to send all your automated emails this way, just your welcome emails. This helps get right into the "primary" inbox to help let your new user know to look out for your future emails.

I also recommend that you personalize your serer-level emails. Not just on the user end but on yours as well. What I mean by that is that instead of your server-level welcome email title reading "Welcome to Acme", Have it say something like: "This Brad from Acme checking in". This will help with your open rates in this scenario.

Bundles. Bundles, Bundles

Here is the thing; Customers love bundles. Why? Because bundles offer value.

Most folks would love to and will jump at a chance to get all they need in one place, for a simple easy-to-understand price.

I am talking about bundles now because as you plan and set up an email marketing system, especially when you begin to automate a whole lot of your messages, you will start to look for ways to get your target audience to open your emails to read or watch a video on what you have to offer.

Just like how we talked about using quality content during our discussion on social media marketing, you will want to think of ways in which you can engage your audience.

This is super important for many reasons.

For one, you'll want as many people as possible to see

your emails in their entirety.

Two, you will want to boost your "opens" to ensure that your messages do not start going into folks' spam folders. And trust me when I say that they will If nobody opens your email messages, and as you continue to send tons of them via automation, your sending reputation could be diminished, which will hurt your delivery rates and could eventually cause your messages to stop going out altogether.

REPUTATION HEALTH

6

Acceptable

Learn to improve

Your sending reputation is probably one of, if not the most important aspect of email marketing. Without an "acceptable" sending reputation your emails will not have success.

Use all available tools to make sure you are presenting value with each campaign. Offering value via bundles, and clearly labeling your emails as such will help boost your email opens and help you sign up more subscribers or sell more of your products and services.

Bundles are pretty easy to set up. The key is to offer complementary products as bundles at slightly discounted prices compared to those products or services being purchased separately.

Amazon does a great job at offering bundles that make sense. Of course, they do so by using AI technology to determine which products their customers are more likely to buy as a bundle.

They also use historical purchase data to help create bundles to offer to their new customers.

I love receiving emails from Amazon offering bundles. I always open those emails to see how I can purchase what I need at a discount.

Tips and Hacks

If you offer your products and services to other organizations, especially other small businesses then you are in a great position to boost your email marketing and email automation responses.

Sure, you can implement this next plan in other circumstances, but this type of strategy works best if you are in the B2B space.

You can provide a great added service to your customers by offering for free an asset that you already possess and probably did not realize it.

Picture this. Let's say you sell an online marketing platform. And most of your customers are small businesses in a particular industry, or various related verticals, you are able to harvest all the data/analytics you have collected over the years of serving that particular niche.

You can spend some time, with the help of a data analyst to create reports and even educational material like online courses to help educate your customers on what works well in their industry and what does not.

I mean, think about it. Who better than you? You have a bird's eye view of their businesses.

You are in a position to notice trends, new issues and developments in that particular industry, etc. You can use the data to create eBooks, reports, articles, etc.

You then want to segment these reports to be sent out automatically to certain relevant lists of your customers.

Doing so will help drive more traffic to your website(s) and help establish brand authority and increase your profit margins.

Synergy and automation

This is a strategy best for those of you who offer different types of products and or services. You can help power your email automation system by upselling and cross selling related products and services.

This strategy should be approached with care and deep analytics. Sure, folks who buy certain things from you will love to know that you have other products and services to offer.

That is if they care about the other stuff you are offering.

Here you will want to use your email marketing platform, if you have a powerful one like Benchmark to carefully segment and customize your list so as to only send out and automate product recommendations that are relevant to your recipients' needs and wants.

Folks who bought fishing gear from you may be interested in knowing that you also have camping gear for sale. Customers who signed up for your social media marketing blog would probably be interested in knowing that they can also signup to use your social media marketing platform.

Automating these kinds of emails will over time create a sales system like no other. You might have to spend some time creating the various reports, lists segments, and automation to get this plan in place, but once you do, all you have to do is to keep adding new emails to your list and wait for your email automation system to do the rest.

CHAPTER SEVEN

PLAN, SEGMENT, PERSONALIZE

Every success story and every win, every victory starts with a plan.

Sure, the plan may not be as clear as you would like it to be when you start, but one is required to "win" at anything you do. And business is no different.

In fact, some would argue that in business, you will find yourself doing the "planning" part of any initiative most of the time.

As small business owners and entrepreneurs, we spend most of our time planning, strategizing, reading reports, meeting with our teams, Lawyers, Accountants, and so on.

You will have to develop a living plan for every aspect of your business. Plans that will need to be changed, tweaked, and updated from time to time.

Marketing and Marketing automation is no different. You need a solid plan to help kick things off. You will need to plan out which marketing channels to use.

Will you look to reach your target audience via social media, Email, SMS Messaging, or all of the above? You will also want to consider who you will want to reach, how to reach them, what to say, how to say it, and so on.

In this chapter, we will look at various aspects of your marketing automation and how to think about them. This section of the book involves taking a holistic look at your marketing automation apparatus and the various ways and strategies available to help with a flawless execution of your overall goals.

Always start with a plan
Always! You do not have to have a perfect, well-thought-out plan when you embark on any new project or in this case, marketing campaign.

Nope! it takes time, experience, and a whole lot of trying and error-ing for a plan to come together. However, you will want to have some idea of where you are going.

It is best to document your plan in some way. This will help you make the necessary changes to it when you need to.

You will also be able to refer to your plan during the course of implementing it and be able to share it with other interested parties.

There is no set standard of what to include in your marketing automation plan.

Most successful plans I have seen in this particular area answers the following questions:

- What is the point of putting an autonomous marketing plan in place?

- Who am I trying to reach with my campaign?

- What value can I offer my target audience?

- What is my ultimate goal? In other words, what do you want folks to do in the end? Do you want them to buy something? signup for your newsletter? make a donation?

Your initial plan should include these questions and your answers to them as you see fit at the time.

Sure, as time goes on you will add some other questions and answers to your plan, but here is a very good place to start.

Know your audience

Here is a very important part of marketing, especially in the realm of automation. For the purpose of this book, keep in mind that most of the ideas I am sharing are meant to help you build a killer marketing automation machine.

One that sends out valuable, relevant campaigns; answers customers questions and converts browsers to customers all while you focus on other aspects of your business. Or perhaps while you are on vacation or tending to the more personal parts of your life.

One key element to successful automation is relevance. You will have to set your marketing automation system up so as to send out messages that are uniquely valuable to your end-user.

This can be tricky since most businesses have thousands, even millions of users and prospects all with varying needs and wants.

The key to helping to improve your "targeting" is knowing your audience.

As part of your planning, you will want create customer personas.

If you only offer your products and services to one particular type of customer, then this will be fairly straight forward for you. For those with a diverse mix of customers, you will want to create separate customer profiles for each type of customer.

Different organizations include different types of information in their customer profiles, but for the most part, your customer profile should include:

Profile name: Creating a catchy, easy-to-remember profile name will help you not only refer back to your ideal customer in shorthand but will also let you and your team keep in mind what type of person(s) you are looking to reach.

Demographic: This part of your customer profile should cover attributes such as age, gender, ethnicity, geography (city, state, county) and members of your ideal customer's household.

Socioeconomic: Here you will want to clearly identify your ideal customer's household income, level of education, profession or vocation, community, and affiliations.

Psychographics: This section of your customer profile should include information about your ideal customer or user's lifestyle, life stage, personality, attitudes, opinion, and even voting behavior

Geography: This includes data related to where (geographically) your ideal customer lives and/or works.

You may choose to include or exclude more profile data in your customer profile depending on the type of business you are in, and the type of customers you serve.

The key is to include any pieces of data that will help you clearly place each customer in a well-defined group.

This will help you target each "type" of customer with only offers they are likely to care about.

Segment for best results

Once you have created your customer or audience profile, it is time to think about how you intend to create well-defined segments.

Customer segments, for the purpose of this book, refers to groups of prospective or existing customers you create to help communicate with said groups in an effective and relevant way. In each segment, you will place prospects or customers that have similar profiles.

When setting up your automated campaigns, whether email, social media or some other form of marketing, keep in mind to provide (through your chosen platform) as much information about each customer or type of customer as possible.

Proceed to segment your audience based on the most relevant aspects of their profiles. Of course, each different type of campaign will have different part(s) of the profile that is relevant.

For example, if you are launching an automated campaign for certain types of customers in your city, you will, above all else target the members of your chosen segment(s) that reside within the city limits.

Hosting a kid's party to showcase your new kiddie line will require that you only target folks on your list (preferably women) who have "Child present" in the household.

Effective audience/customer segmentation will allow you to only send out impactful and relevant campaigns to the folks that are most likely to take the action you need them to take.

Most marketing platforms like Hootsuite and Benchmark will provide all the tools you will need to create detailed audience segments. There are also other platforms out there that will allow you to create rich automated campaigns for social, SMS, email, etc. All in one place.

Examples of such all-in-one marketing automation platforms are Prospect.io and HubSpot. I shall list and talk about a few more of these in the next chapters.

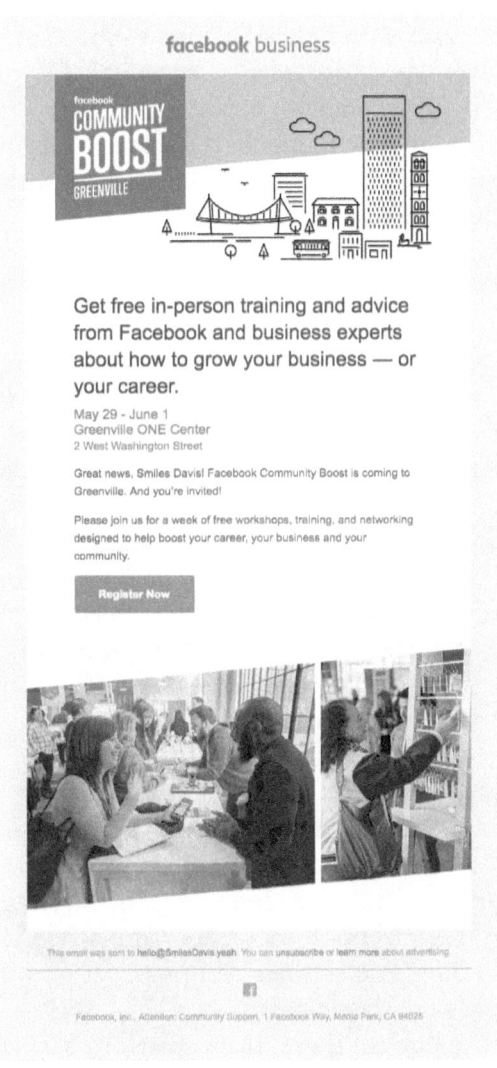

Facebook used user segmentation to invite folks to a community event.

On a more personal level

Beyond creating audience segments, you will want to personalize your campaigns as much as possible, wherever and whenever you can. Use the information gleaned from your target audiences' social media pages to help craft messages that mirror their stated or inferred preferences.

Social media

Most social media platforms go out of their way to collect and share with their advertisers (you) a treasure trove of unique data about their users. Facebook is great at this. The social media giant provides tools that will help you target your audience in many ways

When it comes to location, with Facebook ads, you will be able to reach out to folks in your area, by state, county, city, even by zip code. You will be able to also target folks based on their interests, professions, hobbies, and so much more.

Chatbots, SMS, and more

I use Tidio (https://www.tidio.com/) for chat. I like the system very much. I also use Callhub (https://callhub.io/) for creating SMS campaigns. I also like the Facebook messenger app when it comes to responding to customer and prospect questions on our various Facebook pages.

I mention these three platforms specifically because each allows some level of target outreach and automation.

Tidio for example, allows you to create unique, mission-specific chatbots to help you respond to customers with unique needs.

The system also can help you communicate with your customers and prospects via email and social media in one place.

With these platforms, you will be able to personalize your messages to help create outreach efforts that will resonate with your audience.

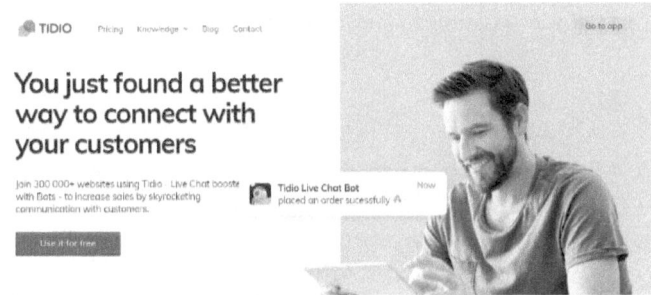

(https://www.tidio.com/)

https://callhub.io/)

Email marketing

Most email marketing platforms will also provide you with the tools you need to help create lists out of lists. This means you will be able to create sub-groups of each of your prospect or customer lists and personalize each message as much as possible.

Most large corporations and other organization that are great at digital outreach will typically personalize the following:

First name: Try to send all your campaigns (when possible) using the first name of your intended target. The "Fist name" marker should also be present in the header of your email campaigns.

Research from Pinpointe marketing found that using a specific personal name can increase email open rates by as much as 35%!

Date of birth: You can personalize emails and other forms of (automated) campaigns using the dates of birth of your customers in many ways.

You can send out automated "Happy birthday" messages and also create discounts with unique discount codes that are sent to your customers on or before their birthdays to let them know that you remembered! And that they can get a special gift seeing as it's their birthday.

This strategy is great if you have a large list of customers, for obvious reasons: You will have folks shopping on your site every single day using birthday codes.

Usage or interaction: Have levels that user must reach to get a discount or some kind of reward?

Enterprise, the car rental company allows you to accrue points based on your rental history. Once you have reached a certain point level, you will be able to apply those points towards a free rental.

This type of reward system, being an Enterprise customer myself, is great for business folks since we tend to use rental cars frequently and are the Company's largest customer segment.

If you do not have such a system in your business, I encourage you to create one.

You will be able to use this as a great way to entice your customers to use or buy more of your products, and more frequently.

Milestones

Create and send out special "Milestone" campaigns. These are awesome at showing customers that you appreciate their business and continued patronage. These types of campaigns are also great for starting conversations about new products and services.

Some common milestones to build your campaigns around may include number of months, or years a customer or client has been with your company and / or certain thresholds the customer may have crossed, as is in the case of Lyft when they let their users know how close they are to a certain number of rides and the reward(s) that await once they reach the next threshold.

Milestone campaigns, when strategically crafted, implemented and automated will allow you to interact with your customers on dates that matter the most to them on an individual basis, thus creating a unique memorable experience for each of them.

Also, these types of campaigns will go a long way to create brand awareness while building goodwill.

This year, we're looking back at a stellar 2017 and your lifetime journey as a Lyft passenger.

18	14	83
Lifetime rides taken	Rides taken this year	Miles traveled this year

2016

When you joined the Lyft community

2016 was the year that a female athlete from the US team won four gold and one bronze medal at the Rio Olympics gymnastics competition.

CHAPTER EIGHT

CHATBOTS, SMS, AND MORE

Sure, some of the marketing platforms and methods we have discussed so far offer the most reliable and widely-used applications through which you are able to tell your brand narrative to the largest audience possible, but besides email and social media, there are various other channels of communication you can use to get your brand messaging out to your target audience.

There are many opportunities to enhance the ROI of these other methods as well including automation.

That's right! Chatbots, Instant messenger applications and SMS platforms all offer ways to anticipate your customers' needs and deliver answers in an automated manner.

Facebook Messenger, when it comes to messenger apps offers the most robust set of features to help you connect with your social media audience and capture leads while providing awesome customer service to your existing customer base in a more natural setting.

In this chapter, we will look at some of the lesser-known modes of communication in today's business environment, and how you can set up various automated workflows to help streamline your marketing and customer service systems.

Automate as much as you can

Automation is key in scaling any marketing system/ campaign. This is vital if you are a solo operator or have a small team. You, more than anyone else understands the limitations placed upon you and / or your team due to the fact that there just aren't enough hours in the day, any day, to get done what must be done.

You always seem to check off one, maybe two of the stuff you need to get done on any given day. But let's be real, most of the stuff you do during the day (as far as customer communication is concerned) are repetitive, right?

I mean, you seem to send the same type of emails, answer the same type of questions via Live Chat, send the same demo over and over again. Does this sound like your life?

Automation is the answer. After reading this book, I want you to take a closer look at all your customer and prospect communications, regardless of how you communicate with your audience, to see which aspects you can automate using the many software applications on the market today.

You can visit the Google Chrome add-on store to see which apps can be used in conjunction with your browser and already existing applications to assure the smooth automation of some of your more routine actions.

Yesware (https://www.yesware.com/), for example can help automate many of your email workflows even from the Gmail environment.

Do yourself a favor and spend this weekend going through all the mundane repetitive tasks you perform day in, day out and see how best you can introduce automation to enhance productivity, consistency, and efficiency and help boost your bottom line.

Yesware (https://www.yesware.com/)

Live Chat

Live chat, the little widgets you can place on your website allowing you to communicate well, "live" with your prospects and customers, have become super advanced over the last ten years.

This legacy technology pioneered by firms like LiveChat Inc. has been transformed into something new and much more useful. I use live chat all day every day. As I mentioned before, I am a fan of Tidio.

We have incorporated their chat system across all our platforms and websites. They and other firms like ZenDesk provide a whole host of tools to help small business folk like you and I connect with our customers and prospects. Tidio, in particular, has over the last five years or so introduced many other features. These features are all aimed at providing their customers with the tools to execute cross-platform communications and automation.

As more companies, even fortune 500 firms like Walmart Inc. Move to reduce the cost of customer service, many are warming up to the idea of providing Live Chat as a primary means of communication. Newer technology firms today barely offer phone support.

Companies like HealthSherpa offer chat and email as the two main ways their users can communicate with them. The latest shift away from live phone support is meant to improve customer service while helping firms all over the world reduce their customer support costs and attract international audiences.

These changes in customer communications have inspired much-needed innovation and user growth in the live chat arena. In fact, according to customer service research firm, Yourchatteam Inc., 51% of consumers prefer live chat to other lines of communication with their favorite brands.

Most consumers say live chat allows them to do other things while they shop and interact with companies. 77% of customers won't shop on a website if there's no live chat option available.

Consumers have finally grown accustomed to using live chat and other voiceless forms of communication when seeking customer service. Experts expect the live chat space to see an 87%

growth over the next few years. As a result, small businesses now have easy access to the most sophisticated live chat tools available as well as options to help automate many communication workflows.

Some of the many tools within the live chat and messenger universe that can help companies improve customer communications while making available open communications lines 24/7 are:

Chatbots

Basically, a chatbot is a piece of automated messaging software that uses Artificial Intelligence and machine learning to communicate with people.

An automated engine embedded in most modern live chat applications has emerged as a primary method through which firms of all sizes all over the world provide continuous customer support. These applications can be comprehensively programmed to handle all sorts of service requests and queries from customers and prospects around the clock and across all time zones.

According to various estimates, over 67% of consumers rely on chatbots for support annually. Approximately 85% of all customer communications will be handled by artificial intelligence by 2020.

Although some consumers prefer to deal with humans when seeking out support, over 40% are indifferent.

Chatbots range in complexity and

sophistication. Some can be programmed to handle simple customer service questions while others can be set up to autonomously handle complex multi-layered customer requests. Whichever option one chooses will be largely dependent on the type of business you are in and what level of support you are looking to depend on your chatbot system to provide to your audience.

The use of chatbots can help you save on your customer service costs while helping to deliver speedy support to your customers.

Canned Responses 2.0

Canned responses are nothing new. If you have ever worked chat support for a big firm, you know these are very useful. These are essentially notes and short answers you save in your system to help you answer some of the more frequently asked questions you encounter when interfacing with your customers.

Most legacy chat applications will offer the ability for users to save these short responses and make them available for use via short keys.

There is a newer version of this handy tool hitting the market. Gmail has unveiled a version of this technology.

Newer versions of canned responses work like this: Artificial intelligence embedded in your chat or email system will, over time learn how you communicate and also scan your emails and chat messages to make suggested responses.

This is meant to help you provide consistent answers to the questions you receive. Although not quite automated, canned responses deserve a mention as it adds to the efficient automation of your customer communications and prospecting activities.

Facebook Messenger

I felt the need to dedicate a whole section of this book to Facebook Messenger. What began as a simple chat application to help Facebook users communicate in real time has emerged as one of the most powerful customer support tools around today.

Facebook Messenger works very well with your Facebook Company page. Now, if you do not have a Facebook page for your company, I strongly suggest you get one. For one, you will be able to take advantage of the many advertising programs Facebook offers through your page.

You will also be able to handle customer support questions by integrating your Facebook Messenger with your live chat application of choice. Tidio, for example, works very well with Facebook Messenger. The Company, Facebook itself offers a neat little app to help you address all your customer support requests, via messenger, on your mobile device.

Have Multiple pages? No problem. The Messenger app helps you communicate with visitors to all your pages from one mobile interface.

Facebook chatbots

A few years ago, Facebook also introduced its very own chatbots via the Facebook Messenger application. So, what are Facebook chatbots? Well, we have already covered the basic premise and functions of chatbots. Facebook's version of this piece of AI exists solely within the Facebook Messenger framework.

Their chatbot is available to all of the 1.3 billion people who use Facebook Messenger on a monthly basis. As a small business owner, however, looking to scale your business via automation, chatbots from Facebook presents a tremendous opportunity for you to do just that.

You should be able to integrate Facebook chatbots into your overall Facebook and social media strategy quite nicely. The key is to find chatbots that will help you streamline and automate your entire communication system, and also to only use other applications that work well with your overall social media automation strategy. At the time of writing this book, Facebook had over 300,000 chatbots available for use.

Facebook Messenger bots for business
Using Facebook Messenger bots will help improve your communications with your customers, and also make your brand available (in a natural way) to the billions of Facebook users around the world. Using Facebook's chatbots, in addition to your Facebook company page, will among other things help you reach a wider audience.

Facebook Messenger is the third most used app in the world, accessed and used by 68% of app users. Consumers are now, more than ever, more comfortable with using Facebook Messenger in ways that transcend just the friendly chat with friends.

A recent survey by Neilson found that consumers feel that Facebook Messenger is the second-best way to communicate with brands. In fact, over 2 billion messages are exchanged between consumers and brands each month.

As it relates to business communications and automation: the main topic of this book, Facebook chatbots provide a means and ways in which you, the small business owner can curate your messages to specifically address the needs of your target audience.

Not only can you communicate with your existing customer base via Facebook messenger and chatbots, but you can also reach out to new users and customers directly through the various advertising programs available within the Messenger universe.

Facebook Messenger can help you, besides the points already mentioned:

- Communicate with your audience directly and inexpensively

- Reignite communications with folks who have gone dormant.

- Identify, nurture and convert new leads

- Handle e-commerce transactions

- Building your very own Facebook Chatbot

Building a Facebook Messenger Chatbot

Facebook, with its wide usage and low barrier to entry, there is an urgent need to make sure you are fully engaged with everyday Facebook users. These folks, whether they use the popular app via mobile or on their Desktop computers, comprise a majority of consumers.

Integrating Facebook Messenger into your live chat and email communication setup will ensure that you are available to capitalize on the with unlimited sales, service and brand marketing potential available on the Facebook platform.

As discussed earlier, you can capture a sliver of the audiences available on Facebook without making any major capital investments to do so. You can easily create your very own chatbot to serve as your automated intelligent - available 24/7 customer service rep/ Brand ambassador. No technical skills required.

Here are a few tools you can use to build your very own Facebook Messenger chatbot according to social media consulting firm Hootsuite:

Streamchat

Streamchat is one of the most basic chatbot tools out there. It's meant to be used for simple automations and autoresponders, like out-of-office replies or "We'll get back to you as soon as we can!" messages, rather than for managing a broader workflow. It's quick to implement and easy to start with if you're just dipping your toes into the chatbot waters. Streamchat also integrates with Hootsuite Inbox using the Facebook Messenger handover protocol.

MobileMonkey

This free tool features a visual chatbot builder for Facebook Messenger with several bells and whistles, including: Q&A triggers, Live Chat Takeover, Chatbot Templates, Custom Attributes, and more. There's also a "Chat Blast" feature, similar to Chatfuel's "broadcasting" feature, that allows you to send messages to multiple users at once.

If you upgrade to a "Pro" plan with Hootsuite, you'll have access to some of the more valuable features, like scheduling, analytics, and drip campaign setup.

PS: MobileMonkey is primarily designed for non-technical users. That means no coding required. It also integrates with Hootsuite Inbox using the Facebook Messenger handover protocol.

ManyChat

ManyChat's interface is one of the least intimidating out there. However, it may be better suited to those making simpler bots—message management can get cumbersome as the conversation gets complex.

On the plus side, ManyChat has plenty of tools that will help *you promote your bot and evaluate user analytics. It's free at first, but after you hit a certain number of subscribers, you'll need to start paying for a Pro account.*

Automat

This is an enterprise-level, fully managed bot provider, meaning you tell them what you want, and they'll build it for you. Their clients include top brands in a range of industries, but especially in retail and CPG (consumer packaged goods) companies. This is probably because their chatbots can catalog and host a view of products within the chat itself, making it a favorite of beauty companies like Vichy, Covergirl and L'Oreal. Automat also integrates with Hootsuite Inbox using the Facebook Messenger handover protocol.

Facebook Messenger for Developers

If you're up for coding your own Messenger bot, Facebook provides a multitude of resources. And they are always working with their developer community to come up with new ideas to improve the user experience. Sephora and Nike, for instance, are currently testing augmented reality camera effects for their customers.

CHAPTER NINE

All-IN-ONE MARKETING AUTOMATION PLATFORMS

In the quest to find the all-inclusive marketing automation software, one just has to do a quick Google search to understand the endless options available on the market. While the options available seem to be endless, and sometimes a bit overwhelming, finding the "right" Marketing automation software application for your business is not an impossible task.

Start by identifying the most important functions that you need in your software product.

WHAT ARE YOUR SPECIFIC NEEDS?

For example, some questions to consider when choosing the right tool for your business are:

- Do you need a CRM or do have your own?

- Does your CRM integrate with your new marketing tools?

- For your email marketing, do you need a tool that sequences your emails, sends different emails to different demographics?

- Does your business need to send out emails to customers based on their interactions with your website or products?

- Do you need a marketing tool that Integrates with social media like Facebook and Twitter?

- Do you need a tool that can schedule to share your content, to your social media contacts, as well as record and organize social media comments on to your CRM?

Answering these questions, helps you to narrow down the most important preferences you need to have in your marketing automation software.

You then need to find one that is also affordable, easy to use and Integrates with your existing collection of software tools. Below are the most popular all-in-one marketing automation platforms on the market today.

ONTRAPORT
https://ontraport.com

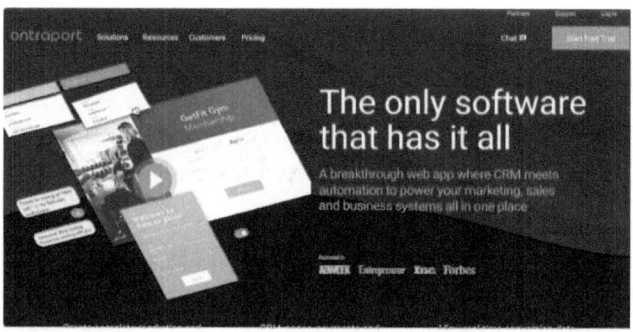

Image Source

Ontraport is an all in one marketing automation

software for entrepreneurs and small business. Their system offers several Important features:

Customer management
Their Customer relationship management system stores customer information tracks online engagement, stores customer clicks and purchase action through campaigns.

Email marketing
Ontraport offers professionally designed email templates for your email marketing. The system also segments your contacts so you can send the right email to the appropriate group either instantly or on a schedule. They offer private IP to improve the accuracy of inbox placement of emails, and the system also removes unresponsive email from campaigns so that your messages can have the most impact.

Landing Pages
The system allows you to create pages that show off your products and services and convince browsers to join your list and/or take a revenue-generating action.

Text Messaging
Send and receive text messages to and from your customers/ contacts for appointment reminders messages, special coupons and sales, product offerings and purchase confirmations.

Pricing

Ontraport offers 4 pricing plans, with different levels of access for the price. The Basic plan starts at 79$ a month, Plus (147$/mth), Pro(297$/month) and enterprise (229$/mth).

SEND IN BLUE
https://www.sendinblue.com

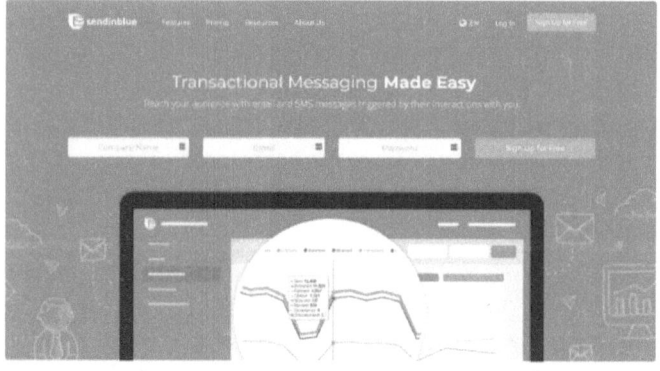

Image Source

Sendinblue is an all in one digital marketing solution toolbox. They offer several tools in their arsenal for your existing customers and to help you acquire new ones.

TOOLS FOR EXISITING CUSTOMERS

Email Marketing
You can design sleek emails using pre-existing templates. You can also segment your contacts so you can market to a more targeted audience and automate your messages to free you up to do other tasks.

SMS Marketing
This feature enables you to communicate promotions and time-sensitive messages more directly to customers.

Live Chat
Their built-in live chat feature allows you to provide customer service and sales support to customers in real time as they browse your site.

Customer management
The Customer Relationship Management tools keep, organize and groups all your customers in one place. Store notes upload relevant documents on customer profiles. Share and assign tasks to other members of your team, attach deadlines and automate emails and contact list management.

TOOLS TO ACQUIRE NEW CUSTOMERS

Landing Pages
Attract new customers by designing targeted pages for each campaign.

Sign Up Forms
Grow your contact list with forms that you can integrate into your existing website.

Facebook Ads
You can launch ads from your account to reach new or existing audiences.

Retargeting
Show your website ads as they browse other websites to bring back and convert to sales.

Pricing
Sendinblue offers 5 packages with varying features and tools depending on the package. They have a free package, Lite (25$/month), Essential (39$/mth), Premium (66$/mth) and an Enterprise option with custom pricing.

ACTIVE CAMPAIGN

https://www.activecampaign.com

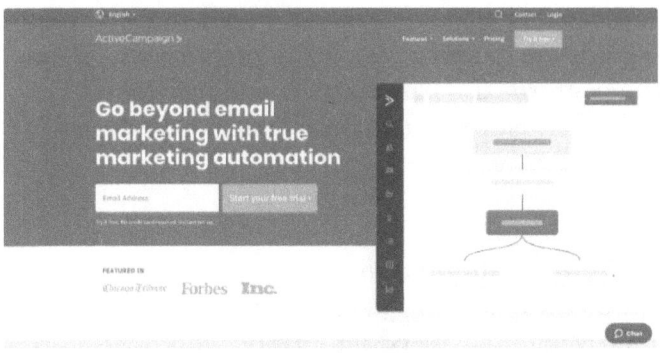

Image Source

Active campaign is an all-in-one marketing solution for small and medium sized businesses. They have a feature-rich, easy to use platform. Their plans are reasonably priced and generous in benefits. Their prices start at $9 a month for their "lite plan", $49/o for the plus, $129/mo for Professional and an Enterprise plan for $229/mth. They offer Email marketing, Marketing automation, and a CRM and compatible with over 200 popular apps.

Email Marketing
With Active Campaign, you are able to create several types of emails to achieve the desired result. You could create automated triggered emails based on a customer action; for example, send a thank you email which is triggered by a customer purchase. You could group your contacts into different segments based on

various characteristics and send targeted emails to different audiences. If one of your business processes is onboarding, you can also set up a series of automated responder emails at predetermined times to guide the customer through a predesigned process. The platform also has reporting and metrics that show the best performing emails and what emails need tweaking.

Marketing Automation
The platform allows you to map out your marketing strategy with the use of automation workflows. An example is illustrated below.

You could also automate workflows in coordination

with other apps. The platform plugs in with other popular apps like Shopify so you could automate remarketing of products that customers were interested in but did not complete the purchase.

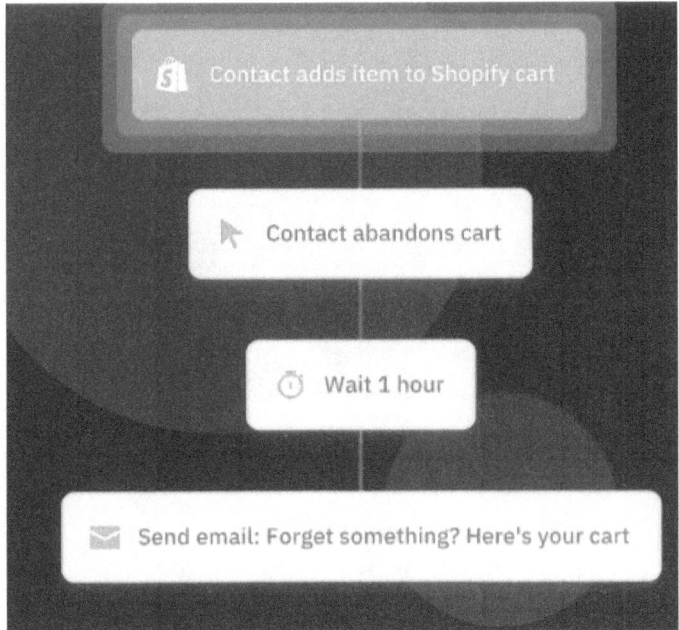

CRM
Organize customer and lead contact information. Manage info while in the field using the CRM mobile app.

DRIP

https://www.drip.com

Drip is a sales and marketing automation platform mostly geared towards eCommerce businesses. They offer 3 plans starting with the basic at $49 a month, Pro at $122 a month and Enterprise whose price varies.

Image Source

Drip offers a suite of tools to help you deliver personalized, timely messages across multiple media channels to drive sales. Some of the tools are listed below.

ECRM

This is a customer relationship management tool that is designed to support online shopping. It records each interaction a customer has with your site, where they click, what products they add to their cart and what they purchased. The system also attaches a tag to each customer based on multiple relevant touchpoints and then uses this information to show the customer relevant personalized marketing.

Above are some examples of the tags generated from customer interactions with your website.

Multi-Channel Marketing

With Drip, you are able to employ email marketing and social media marketing all with the aim of driving sales from one platform. You can start by creating beautifully branded emails from the templates available on the site and show your customer ads on products they might be interested in on Instagram and Facebook.

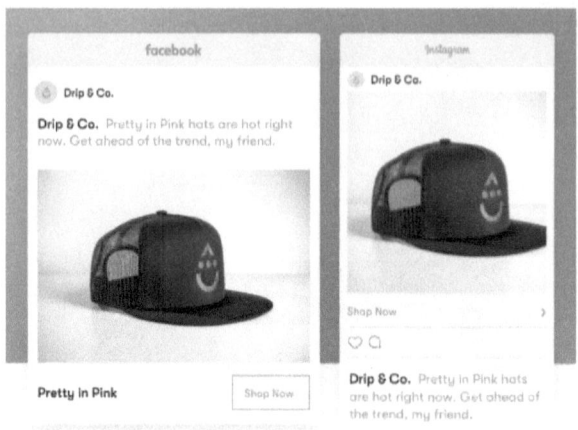

Behavior-Based automation

Drip is intuitive and allows you to design automation workflows based on human shopping behavior. When the customer browses your site, the system is able to send messages to keep their interest in your brand or site and drives up customer engagement.

AUTOMATION INTROSPECTIVA

At this point in human history, it is, I think ok to admit that we have come to depend heavily on our own creations: Machines! It's ok to admit that we look to our inanimate counterparts to complete, sometimes initiate most of our daily duties. Alexa now has the duty of finding information for us, ordering our stuff online, making restaurant reservations, and so on. And she has to do all this while we sit back and expect her to get things right every single time.

Our cars will, and in some instances have become completely self-operating entities. Let's face it, we depend on machines for a whole lot today than we did twenty years ago. I do not really take issue with this new phenomenon. Au contraire mon ami, I love it. I especially love and anticipate great things going forward in the areas of machine learning and automation in business.

I really believe that the small business owner now for the first time in human history has a chance to take on bigger, well-financed firms thanks to AI, automation, and machine learning. She can now get so much done. She can - with a few clicks of the mouse, get her products and service right there in front of the world right next to the big guys.

She can, for the first time compete with firms all over the world. And I mean really compete. For real this time.

ROLE OF SOCIAL

In addition to automation, and some of the other technologies I mentioned here in this book and in others I have written, new technologies like social media and mobile computing have also helped create an atmosphere extremely conducive to the needs and wants of the small business owner and entrepreneur.

Many folks hardly ever stop to think what a godsend social media has been as far as marketing goes. The platforms, with all their other offshoots, have created a situation where anyone with a bit of a budget can position their offerings in front of an engaged global audience.

I have spoken extensively about the opportunities social media presents to the small business owner. I have talked about this topic in this book and others I have written as well. For this reason, I will not bore you with more data to support this argument.

I only bring this up, again, as a reminder of the pivotal role social media plays in marketing automation and marketing overall.

SIRI, ALEXA, AND THE GIRLS

It took me a while to become a believer in these handy tech tools. Maybe it's because most of the folks I know who own them use them in ways that only underscores their own laziness. I know, I am being a bit judgmental, I know, but I cannot help it. I am serious though. Most of my friends who own echo's only use them because they are too freaking lazy to get up and change the channel or find the remote control to do so.

I have, over time realized a whole bunch of ways one can use these new AI assistants in business.

I am also super excited about the news that Amazon plans to release a mobile version of their assistant via earbuds.

There are so many ways in which such a device can be of great import to the small business owner on the go, making deals and taking names.

WELL, THAT'S ALL SHE WROTE

Thank you for making it to the end of my little book. I am hoping you found this body of work to be of some use to you as you look to grow your businesses and brand.

I hope you are able to put to use some of the ideas shared in this book.

Keep in mind that I am by no means an authority on automation or marketing. Nope! I merely seek to share ideas and thoughts gained via years of experience.

I hope to keep writing about the stuff I learn as I continue on this entrepreneurial journey.

ABOUT THE AUTHOR

Frank is Co-Founder of Corvus Web Services, a full-service software services development firm.

He is also a serial entrepreneur with investments and interests in many industries including real estate, eCommerce, financial services, and publishing.

AUTHOR'S OTHER BOOKS

PIXIE DUST:
How to Convince Investors to Invest in Your Business.

This is an opportunity to learn how to attract investors to your business. Learn how to position yourself and your company or business idea to attract Angel Investors and/ or Venture Capital investors. Learn how to produce quality pitch decks, Elegant Elevator pitches, and so much more.

PERSONA:
A Proven Step-By-Step Guide to Identifying and Attracting Profitable Customers to Your New Business.

PERSONA, written by a successful Entrepreneur couple, takes a systematic look at various strategies and methods small business owners and Entrepreneurs can use to build unique businesses and directly market their products and services to potential paying customers. This book will guide you through the process of building effective marketing messages, identifying profitable customers, and so much more.

RECURRING REVENUE:
A Practical Guide to help you launch your very own
Software-as-a-service business

Recurring Revenue Provides any aspiring tech entrepreneur with an easy-to-follow roadmap on how to plan, build and market a Software-as-a-service application. In this book, I share my tips and lessons learned from my years of experience starting and running a 100% subscription-based software services firm. I provide some information on what makes a "Good" app idea, how to build it and ways to market it and get folks to sign up.

EMAIL MARKETING IN A DIGITAL AGE:
Learn how to attract new customers through the

power of Email Marketing and Social Media.

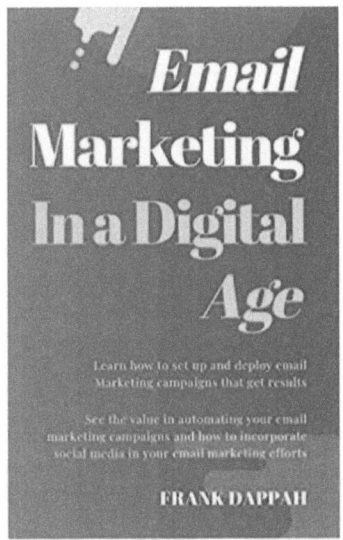

Email Marketing in A Digital Age is a simple, easy-to-read guide on Email marketing. This 150-page book will guide any small business owner or entrepreneur through the process of setting up and deploying effective email marketing campaigns. You will also learn how to incorporate Social media into your email marketing strategy, and many more.

Adventures in

MARKETING
AUTOMATION

Out-of-the-box tips, concepts, and ideas on how to use
Robotics, ***Artificial Intelligence***, *and* ***Automation*** *to*
reach a wider audience.

FRANK DAPPAH

Adventures in
MARKETING
AUTOMATION

Out-of-the-box tips, concepts, and ideas on how to use
***Robotics**, **Artificial Intelligence**, and **Automation** to*
reach a wider audience.

FRANK DAPPAH